GLUTEN FREE MY RECIPE

M.C. NAV

Copyright © 2014 M.C.Nav

All rights reserved.

ISBN: 1497443024
ISBN-13: 978-1497443020

CONTENTS

About the Author (5)

Gluten Free My Recipe (7)

What is Gluten? (8)

Celiac Disease and Gluten Intolerance (11)

Lactose and Dairy Intolerances (12)

Gluten-Free Flour Guide (13)

How to Gluten-Free Your Recipes (15)

How to Dairy-Free and Vegan Your Gluten-Free Recipes (18)

Substitutions Guide (20)

Recipes

Balsamic Pear and Strawberry Salad (24)

BBQ Chicken Pizza (26)

Beefed Up Beef and Potato Stew (28)

Blackened Tilapia and Tartar (30)

Classic Chicken Soup (32)

Cucumber Tuna Boats (34)

Curried Chicken Salad (36)

Fiery Buffalo Sausage Frittata (38)

Grandma's Veal Cutlets (40)

Grilled Cheese and Tomato Soup Makeover (42)

Leftover Stir-Fry (44)

Mexican Layered Lasagna (46)

Millet and Chia Baked Chicken Parmigiana (48)

Mushroom Stroganoff (50)

Oven Fried Cheesy Zucchini (52)

Penne alla Vodka-less (54)

Pepper Steak Pad Thai (56)

Pepperoni Pizza Bagels (58)

Pineapple Fried Rice (60)

Pistachio Pesto Crusted Chicken Breast (62)

Pulled Pork Macho Nachos (64)

Rosemary Pork Chops and Apple Slaw (66)

Shrimp "Don't Skimp on the" Scampi (68)

Sizzling Skillet Chicken Fajitas (70)

Spinach and Feta Chicken Roll Ups with Olive Dipping Sauce (72)

Stuffed Poblano Peppers (74)

Turkey and Cranberry "Not So Chilly" Chili (76)

Turkey Andouille Sausage and Shrimp Gumbo (78)

Very Veggie Lentil Soup (80)

"Wrap me up in Bacon" Shrimp (82)

Extras

Shopping Guide (86)

Glossary of Terms (88)

Measurements and Flour Blends (89)

ABOUT THE AUTHOR

As a child, I never had a large appetite. I was underweight and an incredibly picky eater. I loved a select few, kid-friendly foods – chicken fingers, mac & cheese and mashed potatoes. Any meals that included bread or pasta were my favorites. In my teenage years, as a convenience, I would eat fast food and junk food often. I never thought twice about my unhealthy choices.

Like most kids going through puberty, my body started to react. I put on more and more weight from middle school through my senior year of high school. Even as a two-sport athlete, I struggled to take any of it off. My body image and confidence took a big hit. It wasn't until a required college field hockey physical did I realize that I was forty pounds overweight. My doctor told me it was time to lose some weight.

The summer before my first year in college consisted of field hockey training, workouts and a serious relationship with the gym. My motivation and hard work resulted in a healthy weight loss. Once I was in shape, I didn't find it necessary to change my eating habits.

A few weeks after my twentieth birthday, I began to experience severe abdominal pain after each meal. There was no rhyme or reason, no explanation for the pain. I scheduled an appointment with a local gastroenterologist, and through analysis and blood testing, he diagnosed IBS/Spastic Colon. He prescribed several medications to alleviate the pain, which helped some days, but overall showed no vast improvement.

One Sunday evening, after a day of watching football and indulging in nachos and wings, I was doubled over on the bathroom floor. I knew something had to change. *Could it be my diet?* I heard from a friend in similar digestive distress that a gluten-free diet had alleviated her discomfort. *Hmm, but what is gluten anyway?*

I researched gluten and found my main offenders. *Wait, no cereal? No bagels? No pasta?* For this Long Island, Italian, spaghetti-and-meatball-lovin' girl, this was a nightmare. Nevertheless, I was determined to eliminate anything that caused this intense pain.

When the days of gluten-free turned into weeks, I noticed improvement. My abdominal pain became a rare occurrence. I had more energy, fewer headaches, and my brain fog was nearly gone.

From then on, it became my mission to spread the gluten-free word. I am enthusiastic to share my tips and techniques with those experiencing my pain and frustration. I test the newest gluten-free products, travel the nation to review gluten-free friendly restaurants, and create nutritious and easy gluten-free recipes, as the ones in this book.

GLUTEN FREE MY RECIPE

(GlutenFreeMyRecipe.com)

During my journey to gluten-free, I craved my grandmother's homemade pasta, my mother's famous Chicken Parmigiana and my best friend's warm and chewy chocolate chip cookies. Without my favorite foods, I would have dove off the gluten-free wagon back to pain and suffering. Out of necessity, I developed "Gluten Free My Recipe".

I analyzed my old eating habits and defined unhealthy. I omitted fried foods, excess carbohydrates and sugary snacks. Most people believe any gluten-free food is automatically better for you. That could not be further from the truth. A blueberry muffin or cereal box labeled gluten-free does not make it healthy or low calorie. It can be packed with sugar, saturated fat or processed ingredients.

Next, I dissected my favorite, homemade recipes and made healthy swaps. I replaced whole milk with unsweetened almond milk, fried with baked and whole-wheat pasta with quinoa. The result is this book – thirty delicious versions of my favorite entrée sized meals, all gluten-free and fewer than 500 calories.

On my website, GlutenFreeMyRecipe.com, you can find gluten-free recipes, product discounts, restaurant reviews and fitness tips. I am by no means a certified nutritionist or doctor. I can only share my passion for eating a healthy, gluten-free diet. Today and from now on, I can confidently say, I will always, "Gluten Free My Recipe".

WHAT IS GLUTEN?

Gluten is a protein found primarily in wheat, barley and rye. It is hidden in many products used on a daily basis. Often, naturally gluten-free foods are produced on equipment that also processes wheat. Anytime something gluten-free comes in contact with gluten, it is no longer gluten-free. This is known as *cross contamination*. Do not assume something does not contain gluten, unless labeled "gluten-free". The following lists indicate foods that are off-limits or allowed on a gluten-free diet.

Well-known gluten-containing foods: (unless otherwise indicated)

- Barley
- Beer
- Bran
- Bulgur
- Couscous
- Durum
- Einkorn
- Emmer
- Farro
- Farina
- Graham
- Kamut
- Malt
- Matzo
- Orzo
- Panko
- Rye
- Seitan
- Semolina
- Spelt
- Tabbouleh
- Triticale (Wheat/Rye Hybrid)
- Udon
- Wheat

Sometimes gluten-containing foods: (unless otherwise indicated)

- **Alcohol:** All wines are safe. Many types of liquor, including bourbon, champagne, rum, vodka, whisky, gin, tequila and brandy, are also safe. Be careful with ciders and cocktail mixes. There are also gluten-free beers, ales and hard ciders on the market.
- **Baking Powder:** Some are contaminated during manufacturing.
- **Baked Goods:** Packaged cookies, muffins and cakes will normally contain gluten. Search for gluten-free bakeries in your area or bake your own gluten-free goodies.
- **Breads:** Gluten-free labeled sandwich bread, rolls, dough and wraps are safe for consumption.
- **Broths, Gravies and Stocks:** Most pre-packaged broths, gravies and stocks use all-purpose flour as a thickener.
- **Cereals:** Most cereals are made from gluten ingredients or produced on the same equipment as wheat products.
- **Condiments** (Barbeque Sauces, Ketchups and Mustards)**:** Some bottled condiments are contaminated. Stick to ingredient lists with spices in their pure form and no added sugar.
- **Deli Meats and Imitation Seafood:** Sliced meats, hot dogs, sausages and imitation seafood often contain wheat fillers.
- **Dressings and Marinades:** Many bottled dressings and marinades, like soy sauce or blue cheese salad dressing, contain wheat.
- **Flours:** All-purpose and wheat flours are not gluten-free. Refer to the flour guide for more information (pg. 13-14).
- **Tomatoes, Pasta Sauces and Tomato Pastes:** Some well-known brands are cross contaminated and not gluten-free.
- **Oats:** In their pure form, oats are gluten-free. Generally, they are contaminated. Only buy certified gluten-free oats.
- **Yeast:** All yeast, except Brewer's yeast, is gluten-free.

Some naturally gluten-free foods: (in their pure form)

- **Artificial Sweeteners and Pure Extracts:** Foods containing aspartame, agave, honey, cane sugar, dextrose, stevia, sucralose or vanilla extract are safe.
- **Baking Soda:** Pure baking soda is safe for consumption.
- **Beans:** Lentils, chickpeas, mung and all other beans in pure form are gluten-free.
- **Corn:** Corn flour, corn syrup, cornmeal, masa, polenta, corn vinegar and all forms of corn are gluten-free.
- **Eggs:** Buy organic or cage-free eggs when available.
- **Fresh Meats and Seafood:** Buy meats labeled organic, antibiotic-free or without additives. Select fish labeled farm-raised, wild or without added hormones.
- **Fruits and Vegetables:** Buy organic or locally grown produce, especially those that have thin or edible skin; apples, berries, potatoes, greens, broccoli, peppers, etc.
- **Buckwheat:** Don't let the name fool you. This grain is gluten-free. Use as a hot cereal or try buckwheat pancakes.
- **Millet:** Millet is high in protein, fiber and magnesium. Use puffed millet as a sugary cereal alternative.
- **Quinoa:** Quinoa is a high protein "super-food" that makes an excellent side dish or breadcrumb alternative.
- **Rice:** All rice, rice flour, rice starch, rice vinegar and rice syrups (except brown rice syrup) are gluten-free.
- **Seeds** (Flax, Hemp, Sesame, Sunflower, etc.): Flaxseeds are high in omega-3 fatty acids and fibers. Add a tablespoon of ground flaxseed into waffle or pancake batter.
- **Soy:** Soybeans, soy protein and soy lecithin are safe. Tofu, a popular vegetarian protein alternative made from soy curd, is also safe.
- **Spices:** Spices in their purest form are gluten-free. Some premade spice blends may have gluten additives.

CELIAC DISEASE AND GLUTEN INTOLERANCE

Celiac disease is an autoimmune disease where the immune system has an abnormal reaction to gluten. Depending on the severity of the disease, gluten may cause inflammation or damage to the small intestine. When you are diagnosed with Celiac disease, a doctor should prescribe a gluten-free diet.

If you test negative for Celiac disease, you may still have sensitivity to gluten. Many symptoms of gluten sensitivity mirror Celiac. However, it is difficult for physicians to diagnose sensitivity. Regardless of diagnosis, anyone can benefit from a gluten-free diet.

If you have any of the symptoms listed below, consult your doctor for proper testing. Before your appointment, create a personal food log correlating your food intake to your symptoms.

Symptoms may include, but are not limited to:

- Abdominal Pain
- Gas and Bloating
- Constipation or Diarrhea
- Nausea and Vomiting
- Heartburn or Acid Reflux
- Rashes and Acne
- Fatigue, Joint Pain and Muscle Pain
- Depression and Anxiety
- Headaches or Brain Fog
- Weight Loss

LACTOSE AND DAIRY INTOLERANCES

Lactose intolerance is the inability to digest lactose in a proper manner. Lactose is a sugar present in milk and milk products. You can remove lactose from certain milk products to make them "lactose-free". It is important to understand that lactose-free does not mean dairy-free, and vice versa. Those who have a milk allergy may still react to lactose-free products.

Dairy is any product that contains the milk from cows or other mammals. This includes, but is not limited to, butters, yogurts, cheeses and creams. Any product labeled "dairy-free" does not contain any of these ingredients. Be wary of products labeled "non-dairy". The FDA allows companies to label their products "non-dairy" and still contain milk proteins like whey and/or casein. Make it a habit to check the label's ingredients. It will say "Contains: Milk".

Symptoms may include, but are not limited to:

- Abdominal Pain or Cramping
- Gas and Bloating
- Diarrhea or Bloody Stool
- Nausea and Vomiting
- Hives or Rashes
- Anaphylaxis (Rare)

Unrelated to allergies, some individuals choose to avoid dairy in their diet. Veganism is a practice where individuals do not consume animal products. They follow a strict diet that is dairy-free, egg-free and vegetarian.

GLUTEN-FREE FLOUR GUIDE

Learning the ins and outs of gluten-free flours can be frustrating. No one flour holds all of the properties of all-purpose or wheat flour. However, the combination of a few different flours and starches can act as an alternative. This helpful gluten-free flour starter guide will help you master flour substitution. Consult the flour blends page for additional help (pg.89).

Gluten-free flours: (unless otherwise indicated)

- **Almond Flour/Meal:** Almond flour is low carbohydrate, high protein, and used mostly in gluten-free baking blends. It is excellent for anyone following a "Paleo" style diet. You can make your own by grinding raw almonds in a food processor or spice grinder.

- **Coconut Flour:** Coconut Flour is low carbohydrate and made from coconuts only. It is a great nut-free alternative in recipes that call for nut flours. If used alone, this flour can make your baked goods dry. Use it in combination with other gluten-free flours for an all-purpose flour alternative.

- **Cornmeal:** This is made from grinding down whole corn. There are different colors and levels of grind. Use a fine grind cornmeal in corn muffins and corn bread. To avoid a gritty texture, substitute corn flour.

- **Garbanzo Bean Flour:** Otherwise known as chickpea flour or besan flour, garbanzo bean flour is high in protein and fiber. It is very popular in Middle Eastern, Italian and Indian recipes (like Falafel). Use it in combination with other gluten-free flours for an all-purpose flour alternative.

- **Millet Flour:** This flour is high protein, high fiber and easy to digest. Due to its very mild flavor, it frequently goes undetected. This makes it perfect for bread recipes. Substitute one-forth of all-purpose flour with millet flour for savory baking blends.

- **Oat Flour:** Buy gluten-free oat flour to assure that it was made from gluten-free oats. Adding this flour to baked goods will add a distinct oat flavor. It works best as the main ingredient in cookie and brownie recipes.

- **Quinoa Flour:** Quinoa is one of the most nutritious grains. It is low fat and high protein. Most quinoa flour packages suggest that it can be substituted for half of the all-purpose flour in a recipe. Use this flour to make breads, muffins, homemade pastas or as a coating.

- **Rice Flour** (Brown and White): This is one of the most valuable gluten-free flours. In additional to being a key ingredient in gluten-free all-purpose flour blends, it is excellent for cooking. Use this flour and equal parts fat to make a roux. When breading proteins, coat in white rice flour before dipping in an egg mixture. This will help the breading stick.

- **Sorghum Flour:** This flour is high in antioxidants, protein and easy to digest. It's smooth texture, similar to regular wheat flour, makes it popular for gluten-free baking. Most gluten-free all-purpose flour blends will contain some amount of sorghum. It is best incorporated in cookie, cake and bread recipes.

- **Tapioca Flour/Starch:** Starches are a necessary component of gluten-free blends because they help bind all gluten-free flours. Tapioca starch improves the texture and chew of baked goods. Use tapioca in a flour blend, as a thickener or an alternate to cornstarch.

- **Teff Flour:** Teff is the smallest grain in the world but packed with iron and calcium. Replace half of the all-purpose flour in muffin, waffle and pancake batters with teff flour to add a unique whole-grain taste.

- **Xanthan Gum:** This is a thickening and stabilizing agent. It is an essential addition to baking blends to imitate the properties of gluten. Consult the measurements and flour blends section for quantities (pg. 89).

HOW TO GLUTEN-FREE YOUR RECIPES

Don't throw away your old family cookbooks. More often than not, you can find a gluten-free alternative to any ingredient in your recipe. Be careful. Gluten-free goes far beyond eliminating bread or wheat. Similar to a detective searching for clues, scrutinize labels, pick out the harmful ingredients and replace them with safe ones.

Most grocery stores are stocking their shelves with the newest gluten-free products. On August 2, 2013, the FDA issued a new rule that assures the safety of all foods labeled "gluten-free", "free of gluten", "no gluten" or "without gluten". Now, you can be confident products with those labels are safe for consumption.

After you've become knowledgeable about hidden gluten and filled your kitchen with gluten-free pastas, grains, breads, marinades and flours, you can begin altering your recipes. In particular, flour substitutions can be very tricky. In small amounts, you can substitute all-purpose flour with an equal amount of any approved gluten-free flours (pg. 13-14). Difficulties may arise when you need to replace 1/2 cup or higher of all-purpose flour in a recipe. Refer to the measurements and flour blend guide for help (pg. 89).

The steps I use to gluten-free a recipe reflect a calorie friendly diet filled with lean proteins, organic produce and nutritious grains. If you prefer using butter, sugar, salt, or frying your foods, then feel free. Substitutions can also be made for dairy-free and vegan diets (pg. 18-19). Through trial and error, you'll discover gluten-free versions of your favorite old recipes without compromising the flavor.

Use the following steps to gluten-free your recipe:

1. **List all ingredients in your recipe.**

2. **Assign each ingredient a category; protein, produce, grains, dairy, fats or extras.**
   - Proteins: Meat, Poultry, Eggs, Seafood, Soy, Nuts, etc.
   - Produce: Fruits and Vegetables (fresh, frozen, canned or dehydrated)
   - Grains: Pastas, Breads, Rice, Corn, Oats, Flours, etc.
   - Dairy: Milk, Cheeses, Yogurts, etc.
   - Fats: Butter and Oils
   - Extras: Dressings, Marinades, Stocks, Spices, etc.

3. **Make healthy and gluten-free swaps.** See the substitutions guide for specific examples (pg. 20-22).
   - Proteins: Use lean, low-fat proteins labeled organic, antibiotic-free or farm raised.
   - Produce: Buy locally grown or organic fruits and vegetables.
   - Grains: Use gluten-free grains. Limit the consumption of refined grains and choose whole grains instead.
   - Dairy: Choose dairy products labeled gluten-free and lower in fat.
   - Fats: Cook in healthy oils. Use smaller amounts of butter. Attempt baking instead of frying.
   - Extras: Scrutinize the remaining ingredients. If you are unsure about a product, avoid using it, or contact the company.

Let's take a look at my mother's Chicken Parmigiana recipe (pg. 17). My mom uses non-organic chicken breasts, Italian style breadcrumbs, whole milk mozzarella cheese and homemade, high sodium marinara sauce. It only takes a few small changes to make it gluten-free.

Converting Mama's Chicken Parmigiana (Yields 4 Servings)

Original	Category	Gluten-Free
16 ounces boneless chicken breasts	Protein	16 ounces antibiotic-free, boneless chicken breasts
2 large eggs	Protein	2 organic large eggs or 4 organic large egg whites
2 Tbsps. all-purpose flour	Grains	2 Tbsps. brown rice flour or omit all-purpose flour
1 1/2 cups Italian breadcrumbs	Grains	1 1/2 cups gluten-free breadcrumbs
1 cup shredded whole milk mozzarella cheese	Dairy	1 cup shredded gluten-free part skim mozzarella cheese
2 Tbsps. grated Pecorino Romano cheese	Dairy	2 Tbsps. grated low fat Parmesan cheese
1/2 cup extra virgin olive oil	Fats	1 tsp. coconut oil or gluten-free non-stick spray (for baking)
2 cups homemade marinara sauce	Extras	2 cups homemade gluten-free, no-salt-added marinara sauce (or jarred)

Approximate Nutritional Facts: (Per Serving)

Mama's Chicken Parmigiana

Calories: 756

Total Fat: 44 grams

Carbohydrates: 47 grams

Protein: 45 grams

My Gluten Free Version

Calories: 403

Total Fat: 13 grams

Carbohydrates: 31 grams

Protein: 41 grams

HOW TO DAIRY-FREE AND VEGAN YOUR GLUTEN-FREE RECIPES

After you've eliminated gluten, you might want to make your dish dairy-free or vegan. Similar to the previous section, it only takes a little extra effort to make these alterations.

Use the following steps to dairy-free and vegan your recipe:

1. **List all ingredients in your recipe.**

2. **Assign each ingredient a category; protein, produce, grains, dairy, fats or extras.**
   - Proteins: Meat, Poultry, Eggs, Seafood, Soy, Nuts, etc.
   - Produce: Fruits and Vegetables (fresh, frozen, canned or dehydrated)
   - Grains: Pastas, Breads, Rice, Corn, Oats, Flours, etc.
   - Dairy: Milk, Cheeses, Yogurts, etc.
   - Fats: Butter and Oils
   - Extras: Dressings, Marinades, Stocks, Spices, etc.

3. **Make healthy swaps.** See the substitutions guide for specific examples (pgs. 20-22).
   - Proteins: For Vegans, substitute vegetarian options for animal proteins.
   - Produce: Buy locally grown or organic. Some fruit or vegetables act as a wonderful protein substitute.
   - Grains: Use gluten-free grains. Limit the consumption of refined grains and choose whole grains instead.
   - Dairy: Eliminate any dairy products or replace them with dairy-free alternatives.
   - Fats: Cook in healthy oils. Substitute butter with vegan alternatives. Attempt baking instead of frying.

- Extras: Inspect the remaining ingredients for hidden dairy. If you are unsure about a product, avoid using it, or contact the company.

Let's take another look at my mother's Chicken Parmigiana recipe. The table below illustrates the dairy-free and vegan versions.

Converting Mama's Chicken Parmigiana (Yields 4 Servings)

Original	Category	Gluten and Dairy-Free	Gluten-Free and Vegan
16 ounces boneless chicken breasts	Protein	16 ounces antibiotic-free, boneless chicken breasts	16 ounces tofu, eggplant or zucchini
2 large eggs	Protein	2 organic large eggs	1 Tbsp. egg replacer + 1/4 cup water or 1/2 cup almond milk
2 Tbsps. all-purpose flour	Grains	2 Tbsps. brown rice flour	2 Tbsps. brown rice flour
1 1/2 cups Italian breadcrumbs	Grains	1 1/2 cups gluten-free, dairy-free breadcrumbs	1 1/2 cups gluten-free, dairy-free breadcrumbs
1 cup shredded whole milk mozzarella	Dairy	1 cup gluten-free, dairy-free mozzarella shreds	1 cup rice or soy mozzarella shreds
2 Tbsps. grated Pecorino Romano cheese	Dairy	2 Tbsps. gluten-free, dairy-free grated Parmesan	2 Tbsps. rice-based grated Parmesan
1/2 cup extra virgin olive oil	Fats	1 tsp. coconut oil or gluten-free, dairy-free non-stick spray (for baking)	1 tsp. coconut oil or gluten-free, dairy-free non-stick spray (for baking)
2 cups homemade marinara sauce	Extras	2 cups homemade, gluten-free, no-salt-added marinara sauce (or jarred)	2 cups homemade, gluten-free, no-salt-added marinara sauce (or jarred)

SUBSTITUTIONS GUIDE

Use these substitutions to alter any recipe to fit your dietary tastes or restrictions. More options and product brand reviews are available on my website, GlutenFreeMyRecipe.com

Alcohol-Free Options:

- Gluten-free broths (low sodium chicken, beef or vegetable)
- Gluten-free stocks (unsalted chicken, beef or vegetable)
- Vinegars (apple cider, balsamic, wine vinegars, etc.)
- Water

Dairy-Free and Vegan Options for Mammal's Milk or Creamers:

- Cultured coconut creamer
- Milk made from grains (hemp, rice, oat, etc.)
- Milks made from nuts (almond, cashew, hazelnut, etc.)
- Milks made from seeds (flax, sunflower, sesame, etc.)
- Soy Milk
- Water

Dairy-Free and Vegan Options for 4 Tbsps. Butter:

- Avocado (approx. 1/3 medium avocado)
- 3 Tbsps. unsweetened applesauce + 1 Tbsp. oil/fat
- 4 Tbsps. oil (coconut, grapeseed, sunflower, etc.)
- 4 Tbsps. vegan butter or vegan margarine

Dairy-Free and Vegan Options for Cheese:

- Rice-based cheese alternatives
- Soy-based cheese alternatives

Dairy-Free and Vegan Options for Other Dairy Products:

- Coconut yogurt (unsweetened plain, vanilla, etc.)
- Dairy-free salad dressings
- Vegan cream cheeses (plain, vegetable, scallions, etc.)
- Vegan sour cream (made from soy)

Egg-Free Options for One Large Egg:

- Packaged Egg Replacer
- 1 Tbsp. chia seeds, thickened in 3 Tbsps. of hot water
- 4 Tbsps. pureed tofu and 1 tsp. baking powder
- 4 Tbsps. unsweetened applesauce and 1 tsp. baking powder

Gluten-Free Options for All-Purpose Flour or Wheat Flour (see pg. 89):

- Buckwheat flour
- Cornmeal
- Gluten-free oat flour
- Millet flour
- Nut meals (almond, cashew, etc.)
- Quinoa flour
- Rice flours (brown or white)
- Sorghum flour

Gluten-Free Options for Bread:

- Gluten-free breads (white, cinnamon raisin, "rye", etc.)
- Lettuce wraps
- Mixed greens
- "Paleo-diet" bread (made from coconut)
- Vegan wraps (made from fruit and vegetables)

Gluten-Free Options for Breadcrumbs:

- Gluten-free bread, toasted and made into crumbs
- Gluten-free breadcrumbs
- Gluten-free flours (almond, coconut, brown rice, etc.)
- Ground quinoa

Gluten-Free Snack Options:

- Air popped popcorn
- Corn tortilla chips
- Kale chips
- Potato chips
- Rice cakes
- Seaweed

Gluten-Free Options for Wheat Pasta:

- Bean pastas (black bean, mung bean, soybean)
- Gluten-free grain pastas (corn, quinoa, rice, etc.)
- Gluten-free shirataki noodles
- Rice (arborio, basmati, brown, sushi, white, wild, etc.)
- Spaghetti squash or zucchini noodles
- Quinoa

Nut-Free Options:

- Crushed gluten-free cereals
- Puffed gluten-free grains (millet, corn, rice, etc.)
- Seeds (chia, flax, sesame, sunflower, pumpkin, etc.)
- Toasted unsweetened coconut

Oil Options:

- Canola or vegetable oil (or spray)
- Coconut oil (or spray)
- Extra virgin olive oil
- Ghee (clarified butter)
- Gluten-free stocks (unsalted chicken, beef or vegetable)
- Palm oil
- Seed oils (sesame, sunflower, grapeseed)

Sugar Options:

- Agave or honey
- Cane sugar (granulated, brown, powdered)
- Stevia

Vegan/Vegetarian Options for Animal Proteins:

- Beans (vegetarian canned or dried)
- Nut butters (almond, cashew, pistachio, etc.)
- Nuts and seeds
- Soy-based proteins (tofu, tempeh, etc.)
- TVP (textured vegetable protein)
- Vegetables (eggplant, squash, sweet potatoes, etc.)

RECIPES

BALSAMIC PEAR AND STRAWBERRY SALAD

I have a salad every day with lunch or dinner, which can get monotonous. While chopping my typical salad of romaine lettuce, cucumbers and tomatoes, I glanced at a pear I had bought from a local organic fruit stand. I discovered that pear pairs well with balsamic vinegar. The natural sugars from the fresh fruit counterbalance the tartness of the vinegar.

Approximate Nutritional Information: (per salad)

Calories: 252   Total Fat: 10 grams   Carbs: 37 grams   Protein: 5 grams

Ingredients: (Yields 1 salad)

- 2 Tbsps. balsamic vinegar, separated
- 1/2 medium Bosc pear (or Anjou, Asian), sliced
- 1/2 cup organic strawberries, quartered
- 2 cups mixed greens (romaine, spinach, arugula, frisée)
- 5 grape tomatoes, halved
- 1/4 cup red onion, sliced
- 2 Tbsps. pecans (or walnuts, almonds, cashews), chopped

1. Add the pears and strawberries to a small non-stick pan, on medium heat. Drizzle 1 tablespoon of the balsamic vinegar over the fruit. Cook for 5-7 minutes to allow the fruit to caramelize.
2. Place the mixed greens in a medium-sized serving bowl. Add the tomatoes and red onion. Drizzle the remaining tablespoon of balsamic vinegar. Toss to coat the greens.
3. Once the pears and strawberries are tender, spoon the fruit on top of the bed of greens. Reserve any extra liquid from the pan for additional dressing. (The dressing can be served as is or with a splash of extra virgin olive oil.)
4. Serve hot, topped with chopped pecans. Those following a nut-free diet can substitute toasted unsweetened coconut flakes, sunflower seeds, pumpkin seeds or gluten-free croutons. For additional protein, add four ounces of grilled chicken, ham, turkey slices or grilled extra firm tofu.

Tip: I keep my taste buds satisfied with interesting mustards, obscure spices and different types of vinegars. However, some vinegar is not gluten-free. Malt vinegar is strictly off limits. Depending on the brand, you should be cautious with distilled white vinegar, rice vinegar or flavored vinegars. I use balsamic in this recipe, but you can experiment with different vinegar and oil combinations.

BBQ CHICKEN PIZZA

    Who can honestly say they dislike pizza? Today, pizza toppings go far beyond the normal cheese, mushroom or pepperoni. There's white pizza, baked ziti, veggie and pineapple. There's even a salad pizza. You can choose from thin crust, thick or stuffed with cheese. For this New Yorker, there's nothing better than a simple slice of traditional Brooklyn thin crust pie. That was always enough for me, until I tasted this slice of heaven.

Approximate Nutritional Information: (per 2 slices)

Calories: 435   *Total Fat: 11 grams*   *Carbs: 61 grams*   *Protein: 19 grams*

Ingredients: (Yields 1 pizza or 8 slices)

- 1 (13 oz.) container gluten-free pizza dough
- 1/2 cup gluten-free BBQ Sauce, separated
- 8 ounces antibiotic-free, boneless chicken breasts, cubed
- 1 cup dairy-free mozzarella shreds (or regular mozzarella)
- 1/2 medium red onion, diced
- 1 Tbsp. garlic powder (or 2 garlic cloves, minced)
- *Optional toppings:* 1/4 cup freshly chopped parsley, 2 Tbsps. raw red onion (diced), 2 Tbsps. dairy-free grated Parmesan.

1. Preheat oven to 400° F. Use a rolling pin, or your hands, to shape the premade dough into an approximate 10-inch diameter circle. Sprinkle the top with the garlic powder. Place the dough on a pizza stone or greased baking sheet. Bake for 12-14 minutes or until the dough has started to brown.
2. While the dough is in the oven, start preparing the toppings. Add the red onion, cubed chicken and 2 tablespoons of BBQ sauce to a medium sized skillet on medium-high heat. Cook for 5-6 minutes or until the chicken is fully cooked.
3. Remove the pizza stone or baking sheet from the oven. Spread on the remaining BBQ sauce. Leave a half-inch around the sides without sauce for the crust. Layer on the chicken mixture and sprinkle on the mozzarella. Bake for an additional 6-8 minutes. The pizza is done when the mozzarella has melted.
4. Place on a cooling rack for 5 minutes before slicing. Use a pizza cutter, or sharp knife, to cut 8 equal slices.
5. Serve 2 slices of pizza with a side salad.

Tip: If you make pizza often or love crispy foods, splurge the extra bucks for a pizza stone. You can find one for around $20. It can make your pizza taste like it came straight from the pizzeria. The stone can also be used for oven baked sweet potato fries or crispy flatbreads.

BEEFED UP BEEF AND POTATO STEW

    I hated soup as a child. My mother tried everything to get me to eat stew, but I was stubborn. I rather dig my teeth into something delicious then sip my dinner. After you try this recipe, you'll understand why I outgrew that stage and eat stew at least once a week.

Approximate Nutritional Information: (per serving)

Calories: 397   *Total Fat: 19 grams*   *Carbs: 22 grams*   *Protein: 36 grams*

Ingredients: (Yields 6 servings)

- 2 pounds organic boneless beef, cubed
- 2 cups celery, chopped
- 2 cups carrots, peeled and chopped
- 1 medium yellow onion, diced
- 3 garlic cloves, minced
- 1/4 cup red wine vinegar
- 1 (4 cup) container gluten-free unsalted beef stock
- 1 dozen small red potatoes (or purple, blue), quartered
- 1/4 cup gluten-free organic tomato paste
- 1/2 Tbsp. dried thyme (or 2 Tbsps. fresh thyme, chopped)
- *Optional toppings:* 2 Tbsps. chopped scallions, 1/4 cup dairy-free grated Parmesan.

1. Cook the beef, in half-pound batches, in a large cast iron skillet, or non-stick pan, on high heat. Only sear the beef, do not cook completely.
2. Once the last batch of beef is browned, deglaze the pan with the red wine vinegar. Scrap any beef bits from the bottom of the pan.
3. In a slow cooker, or large pot, add the beef, pan juices, beef stock, onions, celery, carrots and garlic. Bring to a boil. Cover, reduce to simmer and cook for 2 hours. Halfway through, stir in the dried thyme and tomato paste.
4. Add the potatoes and cook for an additional hour. Substituting different potatoes can alter the cooking time. The stew is ready when the potatoes are fork tender.
5. Serve hot with optional garnishes.

Tip: When making stew of any kind, make a large batch (at least 4 servings or more). Store the leftovers in plastic containers that have been split into single-serving portions. The next time you're too tired to cook a healthy dinner, you're just five minutes from a hot and nutritious leftover meal.

BLACKENED TILAPIA AND TARTAR

This dish was inspired by a trip to a popular seafood restaurant. It was the first time I tasted tilapia, and I must confess, it was love at first bite. The fish was light and fresh; I knew I must recreate those flavors in my own kitchen.

Approximate Nutritional Information: (per tilapia fillet)

Calories: 202   Total Fat: 7 grams   Carbs: 8 grams   Protein: 30 grams

Ingredients: (Yields 4 servings)

- 4 tilapia fillets (about 5 ounces per fillet)
- 1 Tbsp. extra virgin olive oil
- Juice from 1 lemon
- 2 tsps. lemon zest
- *Blackening seasoning:* 3 Tbsps. paprika, 1 Tbsp. onion powder, 1 Tbsp. garlic powder, 1 tsp. freshly ground black pepper, 1 tsp. cayenne pepper, 1 tsp. dried oregano and 1/2 tsp. freshly ground sea salt.
- *Tartar sauce:* 2 Tbsps. reduced fat vegan mayo, 1/2 tsp. garlic powder, 1/2 tsp. onion powder, 1 Tbsp. of no-sugar-added sweet relish and the juice from 1/2 lemon.

1. Preheat oven to 425° F. Line a baking sheet with foil.
2. Coat the tilapia fillets completely with extra virgin olive oil. Squeeze the lemon over the tops.
3. Combine all of the blackening spices in a small bowl. Sprinkle a small amount of seasoning on one side the fillets. Place the sprinkled side down and pack the remaining seasoning on the tops of the fillets.
4. Bake for 17-20 minutes. Turn your oven's broiler to high. Broil for 5-7 additional minutes to brown the seasoning. To avoid the fillets from falling apart, use a spatula and gently move the fish to a serving dish.
5. Add all tartar sauce ingredients into a small mixing bowl. Stir to combine. For best results, refrigerate before serving.
6. Serve tilapia with tartar sauce and your favorite steamed vegetable.

Tip: Create your own blackening seasoning. Premade spice blends are usually filled with salt and lack the essential spices. Test your spice blend in a small batch. When you're satisfied, make a larger batch and store it in an airtight container or jar, handy for your next meal.

CLASSIC CHICKEN SOUP

I've been told that chicken soup can cure the common cold. Perhaps it's the placebo effect, but studies show chicken soup speeds up recovery. This soup has soothed even my worst sore throats and comforted me on a cold winter's day.

Approximate Nutritional Information: (per serving)

Calories: 157   Total Fat: 3 grams   Carbs: 12 grams   Protein: 21 grams

Ingredients: (Yields 4 servings)

- 1 (4 cup) container gluten-free low sodium chicken broth
- 1 Tbsp. extra virgin olive oil
- 16 ounces antibiotic-free, boneless chicken breasts
- 2 cups celery, chopped
- 2 cups carrots, chopped
- 1 medium yellow onion, diced
- 1 tsp. freshly ground black pepper, separated
- 1/4 tsp. freshly ground sea salt
- *Optional toppings:* 1/4 cup dairy-free grated Parmesan, 1 tsp. hot sauce.

1. Heat the olive oil in a large pot on medium heat. Add the onions, carrots and celery. Sauté for 5-7 minutes. Add the chicken broth and 1/2 tsp. of black pepper. Bring to a boil.
2. Cover, reduce heat to simmer and cook for 60-90 minutes, until the vegetables are fork-tender.
3. Heat a cast iron grill pan, or non-stick pan, to high heat. Season the chicken breasts with sea salt and the remaining black pepper. Cook for 4-5 minutes on each side. Once cooked, chop into bite size pieces.
4. Add the grilled chicken to the pot and simmer for an additional 15-20 minutes.
5. Serve hot with optional toppings.

Tip: Even when I find a healthy, gluten-free soup, I don't enjoy the texture of the chicken and the mushy vegetables. This is precisely the reason I grill the chicken prior to adding it in this recipe. The pre-grilled chicken is the perfect contrast to the tender al dente vegetables and its char gives the soup a unique, smoky flavor.

CUCUMBER TUNA BOATS

One of my fondest childhood memories with my mother is a thing we liked to call, "Finger Food Night". Instead of cooking a huge dinner, we would pick out a ton of little finger foods from the grocery store. We bought crackers, bagel chips, soft cheeses, olives, artichokes, pickles and a can of tuna. I would devour everything but the tuna. It took some time, but I finally created a tuna dish that I enjoy.

Approximate Nutritional Information: (per serving)

Calories: 159   Total Fat: 8 grams   Carbs: 14 grams   Protein: 15 grams

Ingredients: (Yields 1 serving)

- 2 mini cucumbers
- 6 grape tomatoes (or cherry), halved
- 1 (2 oz.) pouch white albacore tuna in water (or canned tuna in water)
- 1 large celery stalk, finely chopped
- 2 Tbsps. red onion, finely chopped
- 1 tsp. Dijon mustard
- 1/2 Tbsp. reduced fat vegan mayo
- 1 tsp. fresh dill, finely chopped (or 1/2 tsp. dried dill)
- 1/2 tsp. freshly ground white peppercorns
- *Optional:* 2 Tbsps. white wine vinegar

1. In a small mixing bowl, add the tuna, celery, red onion, Dijon mustard, vegan mayo, dill and white pepper. Stir to combine and set aside. For a thinner dressing, add a splash of white wine vinegar.
2. Slice the mini cucumber long-ways. Take a small spoon and remove the inside, leaving only one centimeter of cucumber left on the skin.
3. Portion one-fourth of the tuna salad into each cucumber half. Slice the tomatoes in half and place them cut side down on top of the tuna salad. Fit three on each cucumber.
4. Serve with gluten-free crackers and pickle chips.

Tip: I prefer tuna in single-serving pouches, instead of cans, because they don't taste like aluminum. They are perfect for on-the-go lunches. Don't throw away the cucumber centers. Use them in a cucumber salad. Combine 1 cup sliced cucumbers, the leftover cucumber centers, 1/4 cup sliced red onion, 1/4 cup white wine vinegar and 1/2 tsp. freshly ground sea salt. For best results marinate in the refrigerator overnight.

CURRIED CHICKEN SALAD

I realize curry spices in chicken salad sounds a little bizarre. Honestly, that's what I thought before I tasted a similar salad at a healthy cafe. I fell in love with their homemade dressing made with vegan mayo. I expanded on their dish, cut out some of the excess fat and calories for a clean and fresh meal.

Approximate Nutritional Information: (per serving)

Calories: 272   Total Fat: 12 grams   Carbs: 15 grams   Protein: 27 grams

Ingredients: (Yields 4 servings)

- 16 ounces antibiotic-free, boneless chicken breasts
- 2 large celery stalks, diced
- 1/2 cup carrots, shredded
- 1/4 cup raisins (dark or golden)
- 2 Tbsps. raw slivered almonds (or chopped walnuts)
- 1/2 cup reduced fat vegan mayo (or light mayo)
- Gluten-free non-stick spray
- *Mild curry spice*: 1 Tbsp. turmeric, 1/2 tsp. freshly ground sea salt and 1 tsp. of each spice; ground coriander, ground cumin, ground cardamom, ground ginger and freshly ground white peppercorns.

1. Preheat oven to 400° F. Place the chicken on a baking sheet lined with foil and coated with non-stick spray. Bake 20-25 minutes, or until the chicken is cooked to temperature. [The USDA indicates that chicken is safe for consumption with an internal temperature of 165° F.]
2. Add all mild curry spices in a medium bowl. Stir to combine.
3. Remove the chicken from the oven. Once it's cooled, chop into bite size cubes. Add the chicken, celery, carrots and vegan mayo to the bowl and coat completely with curry spice mixture.
4. To keep the texture of your almonds and raisins, add them right before you plan on serving.
5. Serve over mixed greens or on two slices of toasted gluten-free bread.

Tip: I add 1/4 tsp. of cayenne pepper to my mild blend for a spicier curry. Create your own curry to control the sodium and heat levels. Blend a few variations using different spice measurements. Once you've perfected your blend, make a large batch and store it in an airtight container or jar for future use.

FIERY BUFFALO SAUSAGE FRITTATA

You can never go wrong with breakfast for dinner. Eggs are versatile and compliment many different flavors. I like to set up a "frittata bar", with various proteins, cheeses and sneak in a few fun vegetables. This is a great way to involve your guests or your kids. You can bake frittatas in single-serving size dishes to accommodate each person's tastes.

Approximate Nutritional Information: (per serving)

Calories: 167   Total Fat: 6 grams   Carbs: 7 grams   Protein: 22 grams

Ingredients: (Yields 4 Servings)

- 2 gluten-free buffalo chicken sausage links
- 2 organic large eggs
- 1 1/2 cups liquid egg whites
- 1/2 cup red onion, chopped
- 1 garlic clove, minced
- 2/3 cup dairy-free cheddar shreds (or regular cheddar)
- 1/2 tsp. freshly ground black pepper
- 1/2 tsp. garlic powder
- 1/2 tsp. onion powder
- Coconut oil spray
- *Optional topping:* 1 Tbsp. fresh flat-leaf parsley, chopped

1. Preheat oven to 450° F. Heat a medium sized non-stick pan to medium heat. Coat the pan with coconut oil spray and add the fresh garlic and red onions. Cook for 4-5 minutes.
2. While the garlic and onions are cooking, slice the sausage links into nickel-sized pieces. Add them to the pan and brown each side.
3. Whisk the eggs in a small bowl. Add the liquid egg whites and spices. Whisk until well combined.
4. Add the egg mixture to an 8-inch diameter, circular baking dish, coated with coconut oil spray. Add the sausage, garlic and onion mixture. Sprinkle the cheddar shreds over top.
5. Bake for 15-20 minutes until the eggs are fully cooked, and the edges are browned.
6. Cut the frittata into four equal slices and top with extra freshly chopped parsley.
7. Serve with unsweetened ketchup or buffalo wing sauce and your favorite gluten free toast.

Tip: I love crust around my frittata. For the last five minutes, I change the oven to high broil. This will brown the cheddar and create a crispier crust.

GRANDMA'S VEAL CUTLETS

When I was in elementary school, my papa would pick me up at the end of the school day, and we would walk home together. When we entered the house, my grandma would be prepping for dinner. If we were lucky, she would be pounding out cutlets, making our all time favorite meal - veal cutlets, mashed potatoes and sweet peas. Sometimes I'll cook this dish just for the warmth and comfort of those wonderful memories.

Approximate Nutritional Information: (per 4 oz. veal)

Calories: 222   Total Fat: 6 grams   Carbs: 12 grams   Protein: 27 grams

Ingredients: (Yields 4 servings)

- 16 ounces organic veal cutlets
- 1 cup gluten-free breadcrumbs
- 2 organic large eggs
- 1 Tbsp. dried parsley (or 2 Tbsps. fresh parsley, chopped)
- Gluten-free non-stick spray
- *Mushroom gravy:* 1 Tbsp. vegan butter (or unsalted butter), 1 Tbsp. white rice flour (or brown rice flour), 2 cups white or cremini mushrooms (sliced), 1 medium yellow onion (diced), 1 garlic clove (minced), 2 cups unsalted chicken stock and 1 tsp. freshly ground black pepper.

1. Place veal in between two pieces of plastic wrap. Use a meat tenderizer to pound each piece very thin (or ask your butcher to pound them). Repeat for all cutlets.
2. Preheat oven to 450° F. Line a baking sheet with foil and coat with non-stick spray. In a small bowl, whisk the eggs. In a medium bowl, combine the breadcrumbs and parsley.
3. Dip each cutlet into the egg, coat completely with breadcrumb then place on the baking sheet. Repeat the process for all veal cutlets.
4. Cook for 6-8 minutes, flip and cook an additional 5 minutes. Turn your oven's broiler function on high and cook until browned.
5. To make the gravy, melt butter in a medium non-stick pan on low heat. Add the flour and whisk constantly until smooth. Add the onions, garlic and mushrooms and cook for 2 minutes. Add the chicken stock and bring to a boil. Cover, reduce heat to a simmer and cook until thick.
6. Serve veal cutlets with optional mushroom gravy.

Tip: To avoid caked breadcrumbs on your fingers, use one hand for the wet ingredients and the other hand for the dry. Similar to an assembly line, use your left hand to dip the veal into the egg and the other hand to coat with breadcrumbs.

GRILLED CHEESE AND TOMATO SOUP MAKEOVER

Grilled cheese and tomato soup... I can't think of a more iconic pairing. Dipping a buttery, toasty sandwich into a sweet, warm soup is my idea of perfection. How can I possibly make it any better? Some chopped fresh basil and juicy grilled chicken did the trick.

Approximate Nutritional Information: (per serving of soup and one Panini)

Calories: 473   Total Fat: 10 gram   Carbs: 61 grams   Protein: 46 grams

Ingredients: (Yields 4 servings)

- 2 (28 oz.) cans gluten-free, no-salt-added crushed tomatoes
- 1 (4 cup) container gluten-free unsalted chicken stock
- 2 cups fresh basil leaves, chopped
- 1 medium yellow onion, chopped
- 4 garlic cloves, minced
- 1/4 tsp. red pepper flake
- Gluten-free vegetable oil spray
- 16 ounces antibiotic-free, boneless chicken breasts, pre-grilled
- 8 slices gluten-free bread
- 4 slices dairy-free Swiss (or regular Swiss slices)
- 4 slices beefsteak tomato, cut thick
- 4 large romaine hearts
- Gluten-free non-stick butter spray

1. To make the tomato soup, add the garlic and onions to a large pot on high heat. Coat with vegetable oil spray and cook for 4-5 minutes. Add the chicken stock, crushed tomatoes, chopped basil and red pepper flake. Bring to a boil. Cover, reduce heat to simmer and cook for 30 minutes.
2. Preheat a Panini press. If you are working with frozen bread, thaw completely. Between the two slices of bread layer Swiss, lettuce, chicken and tomato. Spray the press with butter spray and toast for 5-6 minutes.
3. Serve one Panini with one serving of tomato soup, topped with extra freshly chopped basil.

Tip: If you don't own a Panini press, cook the sandwich in a large pan on medium heat. Put a plate on top and weigh it down with a heavy can. Cook each side until browned. Sometimes I'll add mustard to the sandwich before I grill it, to warm and melt the condiment.

LEFTOVER STIR-FRY

This stir-fry encompasses all of my favorite vegetables and flavors into one meal. The water chestnuts, in particular, give crunch to each bite. What's the best part about this dish? You use the leftover vegetables in your refrigerator and don't have to spend $20 for takeout.

Approximate Nutritional Information: (per serving)

Calories: 422   Total Fat: 7 grams   Carbs: 33 grams   Protein: 55 grams

Ingredients: (Yields 4 servings)

- 16 ounces pre-grilled antibiotic-free, boneless chicken breasts
- 1 Tbsp. vegetable oil (or canola, peanut)
- 2 cups gluten-free unsalted chicken stock
- 1 (8 oz.) package black bean spaghetti
- 2 cups broccoli, chopped
- 1 medium yellow onion, diced
- 2 garlic cloves, minced
- 1 medium red bell pepper, diced
- 1 cup carrots, shredded
- 1 (1 cup) container whole water chestnuts
- 1/4 cup gluten-free reduced sodium soy sauce

1. Cook the spaghetti according to the package's instructions.
2. Heat the vegetable oil in a wok, or large pan, on medium-high heat. Add the garlic and onions. Cook for 3-4 minutes before adding the bell pepper, broccoli, carrots and water chestnuts. Pour in the chicken stock. Cover, reduced heat to medium and cook for 8-10 minutes, until the vegetables are tender.
3. Slice the pre-grilled chicken breasts into strips. Add the chicken and soy sauce to the vegetables. If more liquid is required, add extra chicken stock.
4. Add the drained spaghetti to the wok. Stir to combine.
5. Serve in a large bowl with additional soy sauce or hot sauce drizzled overtop.

Tip: Try different gluten-free pastas brands and shapes. I find my favorite brands through experimentation. In particular, black bean spaghetti is packed with a ton of protein and excellent for a post-workout meal.

MEXICAN LAYERED LASAGNA

Some of my recipes evolve from the peculiar ingredients left in my kitchen. After I had bought brown rice lasagna noodles from my local health market, I dug through my cabinets to find ingredients different from the ones in typical lasagna. A can of organic black beans, corn kernels and a jar of salsa... I put them all together, and it was crazy enough to work.

Approximate Nutritional Information: (per serving)

Calories: 464   Total Fat: 8 grams   Carbs: 34 grams   Protein: 37 grams

Ingredients: (Yields 4 servings)

- 16 ounces antibiotic-free, ground chicken breast
- 6 brown rice lasagna pasta sheets
- 1 (15 oz.) can organic black beans
- 1/2 cup no-salt-added corn kernels
- 1/4 cup dairy-free Mexican shreds (or 1/4 cup regular cheddar)
- 1 (16 oz.) jar organic medium salsa
- *Spices:* 2 tsps. chili powder, 1 tsp. paprika, 1 tsp. ground cumin and 1/4 tsp. cayenne pepper.
- *Toppings:* 1 jalapeno (sliced), 1 plum tomato (diced), 1/2 cup large pitted black olives (sliced), 2 Tbsps. dairy-free sour cream and 1 medium scallion (chopped).

1. Preheat oven to 400° F. Cook the lasagna sheets according to the package's instructions. Lay the cooked sheets onto paper towels to dry. Drain and rinse the black beans with water.
2. In a large non-stick pan, brown the ground chicken on medium-high heat. Add all the spices to the pan.
3. Spread a third of the jar of salsa in the bottom of a 9x13-inch baking dish. Arrange three sheets lengthwise over the salsa. Spread with half the chicken mixture. Layer on half the black beans and 1/4 cup corn kernels. Spoon over another third of the jar of salsa. Repeat steps for another layer.
4. Top with the Mexican shreds and cover with foil. Bake for 30-35 minutes. Remove the foil and cook for an additional 10-15 minutes to brown the top.
5. Pile on the toppings. Slice into 4 equal squares.
6. Serve hot with extra salsa and dairy-free sour cream.

Tip: This recipe is perfect for alterations. Pick your favorite protein; turkey, pork, beef, bison, ostrich or tofu. Swap out black beans for refried, pinto or kidney. Leave the seeds in the jalapenos for extra spice. Cover with your favorite dairy-free cheese alternative or crushed corn tortilla chips.

MILLET AND CHIA BAKED CHICKEN PARMIGIANA

My mom is famous among my friends for her delicious chicken parm recipe, which is why I was hesitant to attempt a gluten-free version. After a family party, and more rave reviews, I yearned for a taste of her home style cooking, and figured I'd give it a shot. Baked instead of fried, this dairy-free rendition isn't my mom's, but certainly a very close second.

Approximate Nutritional Information: (per 4 oz. chicken)

Calories: 290   Total Fat: 10 grams   Carbs: 20 grams   Protein: 36 grams

Ingredients: (Yields 4 servings)

- 4 slices millet & chia seed gluten-free bread (or gluten-free white bread)
- 16 ounces antibiotic-free, boneless chicken breasts
- 2 organic large eggs
- 1/2 cup dairy-free mozzarella shreds
- 2 tsps. dairy-free grated Parmesan
- 3/4 cup gluten-free jarred marinara sauce
- 1 Tbsp. dried basil (or 2 Tbsps. fresh basil, chopped)
- Gluten-free non-stick spray

1. Preheat oven to 450° F. Remove any visible fat from the chicken breasts and cut them into thin slices.
2. Toast the bread and set aside to cool. Use a food processor to pulse into breadcrumbs. In a small bowl, add the breadcrumbs and dried basil. Stir to combine.
3. Whisk the eggs in another small bowl. Line a baking sheet with foil and coat with non-stick spray. Dip a slice of chicken into the egg then coat completely with the breadcrumb mixture. Place onto the baking sheet and repeat the process for each piece of chicken.
4. Bake for 10 minutes, flip and bake until crispy.
5. Sprinkle each with mozzarella and top with marinara sauce. Turn oven to broil and cook for 5 minutes to melt the mozzarella.
6. Remove from the oven and finish with a sprinkle of dairy-free grated Parmesan.
7. Serve with gluten-free spaghetti tossed in the remaining marinara sauce.

Tip: If you don't own a food processor, add the toast to a plastic baggie and use the flat side of a meat tenderizer, or heavy can, to break into crumbs. If the toast is still warm, you will end up with soggy breadcrumbs. Don't throw away old, stale bread - make breadcrumbs.

MUSHROOM STROGANOFF

It's a challenge to take recipes I see on television, in a magazine or old cookbook and modify it to my dietary restrictions. For this recipe, I transformed the fattening celebrity chef version into a nutritional, but still flavorful dish. Mine is 120 calories less per serving, half the fat, and of course, gluten-free.

Approximate Nutritional Information: (per serving)

Calories: 396   Total Fat: 11 grams   Carbs: 70 grams   Protein: 8 grams

Ingredients: (Yields 4 servings)

- 1 (9 oz.) bag gluten-free egg noodles
- 2 Tbsps. vegan butter (or unsalted butter)
- 5 large portabella mushrooms, julienned
- 2 Tbsps. scallions, chopped
- 1 Tbsp. brown rice flour (or white rice flour, cornstarch)
- 2 cups gluten-free unsalted vegetable stock
- 1/2 cup dairy-free sour cream (or light sour cream)
- 1 tsp. freshly ground black pepper
- 1/4 tsp. freshly ground sea salt

1. Cook the egg noodles according to the package's instructions.
2. Melt the butter in a medium-sized saucepan on medium heat. Add the mushrooms and salt. Sauté for 5-6 minutes until the mushrooms are golden brown.
3. Stir in scallions, reserving some for garnish. Cook an additional 2-3 minutes before adding the flour. Stir until the flour is completely incorporated with the liquid, to create a roux.
4. Deglaze the pan with the vegetable stock and remove any browned bits from the bottom of the saucepan. Turn the heat down to a simmer. Cook, uncovered, for an additional 12-15 minutes.
5. Stir in the sour cream, black pepper and sea salt. Add drained noodles and coat well with the mixture.
6. Serve hot, topped with the leftover chopped scallions.

Tip: Make sure to cook down the mushrooms. This will make them tender and resemble beef flavors. If you don't follow a vegan or vegetarian diet, you may substitute the vegetable broth for beef broth. If you tolerate dairy in your diet, use light sour cream and unsalted butter.

OVEN FRIED CHEESY ZUCCHINI

I have a few vegetarians in my family. My aunt's popular Eggplant Parmesan dish always looked so appetizing. After one bite, my mouth itched, and my lips swelled with hives. No more eggplant for me. Luckily, I'm not allergic to the versatile zucchini.

Approximate Nutritional Information: (per serving)

Calories: 208   Total Fat: 6 grams   Carbs: 22 grams   Protein: 14 grams

Ingredients: (Yields 4 servings)

- 16 ounces yellow zucchini squash
- 1 cup gluten-free, no-salt-added tomato sauce
- 1 cup gluten-free breadcrumbs
- 1 cup dairy-free mozzarella shreds
- 2 tsps. dairy-free grated Parmesan
- 2 organic large eggs
- 1 tsp. dried parsley
- Gluten-free non-stick spray
- Freshly ground sea salt

1. Preheat oven to 400° F. Peel the zucchini. Use a mandolin, or vegetable slicer, to cut vertical thin strips. To remove acidity, sprinkle both sides of each slice lightly with sea salt and let sit on paper towels for 3-5 minutes. Pat excess moisture with more paper towels.
2. Whisk the eggs in a medium bowl. In another large bowl, add the breadcrumbs and dried parsley. Stir to combine.
3. Line a baking sheet with foil and coat with non-stick spray. Dip a zucchini slice in the egg mixture then coat completely with breadcrumbs. Place on the baking sheet and repeat for all slices.
4. Bake for 10-12 minutes, flip then bake until golden brown. Sprinkle each with mozzarella and top with tomato sauce. Turn oven to broil and cook for 5 minutes to melt the mozzarella.
5. Serve zucchini topped with dairy-free grated Parmesan and a side of spaghetti squash tossed in the remaining tomato sauce.

Tip: Ever wonder what to do with that leftover egg mixture and breadcrumbs? My grandma combined them, made a patty and fried them in oil. Combine any leftover egg with the gluten-free breadcrumbs and bake alongside the zucchini. Dip those patties in a side of warm tomato sauce. Yum!

PENNE ALLA VODKA-LESS

When I was ten-years-old, I asked my mom to make me penne alla vodka for dinner. She agreed but soon realized she didn't have vodka in the house. She altered the recipe and invented her own delicious creation. It instantly became a family favorite and was the first recipe she taught me to cook. I changed it one more time.

Approximate Nutritional Information: (per serving)

Calories: 355   Total Fat: 11 grams   Carbs: 60 grams   Protein: 7 grams

Ingredients: (Yields 4 servings)

- 1 (8 oz.) box quinoa penne pasta (or any gluten-free penne)
- 1 (24 oz.) jar gluten-free marinara sauce (or 3 cups homemade marinara sauce)
- 1/4 cup dairy-free grated Parmesan, separated
- 1/2 cup coconut creamer
- 1 tsp. coconut oil
- 2 Tbsps. vegan butter

1. Cook the penne according to the package's instructions.
2. Melt the butter and coconut oil in a large saucepan on medium heat. Be careful not to brown the butter and oil, or it will taste bitter. Add the marinara sauce and bring to a slow boil.
3. Turn the heat down to simmer. Add the coconut creamer and grated Parmesan, reserving some Parmesan for garnish. Stir well to combine. Let simmer, uncovered, for 4-5 minutes.
4. Add the drained penne to the saucepan and coat well with the sauce. Cover and simmer for an additional 4-5 minutes, until the sauce thickens. For a thicker sauce, add a ladle full of starchy pasta water and simmer for 5 additional minutes.
5. Serve hot, topped with the remaining grated Parmesan and my Millet & Chia Baked Chicken Parmigiana (pg. 48).

Tip: If you can tolerate dairy or lactose, try my mom's version of this dish. Melt the butter and add a splash of extra virgin olive oil. Add 3 cups of homemade sauce and about a pint of light cream. Sprinkle in a handful of grated Pecorino Romano cheese. Simmer, let thicken and toss in your favorite gluten-free penne pasta. Non-vegetarians can add chopped chicken, ham, bacon, pancetta or prosciutto for extra protein.

PEPPER STEAK PAD THAI

I love Pad Thai! My eyes lit up when I saw Pad Thai rice noodles, made from just rice flour and water, in the grocery store. Some Pad Thai dishes are made with eggs and shrimp, but instead, I opted for a tender cut of organic sirloin steak.

Approximate Nutritional Information: (per serving)

Calories: 386   Total Fat: 4 grams   Carbs: 52 grams   Protein: 32 grams

Ingredients: (Yields 4 servings)

- 16 ounces organic sirloin steak
- 1 (8 oz.) box pad Thai rice noodles
- 1 medium green bell pepper, diced
- 1 medium yellow onion, diced
- 2 garlic cloves, minced
- 2 broccoli crowns, chopped
- 1 cup white mushrooms, sliced
- 1 cup gluten-free low sodium chicken broth
- 1/4 cup gluten-free Szechuan sauce (or gluten-free reduced sodium soy sauce)
- 1 tsp. freshly ground black pepper
- *Optional toppings:* 1 Tbsp. chopped scallions, 1 Tbsp. unsalted peanuts, 1/4 cup bean sprouts, 1 tsp. Sriracha hot sauce.

1. Soak the rice noodles in warm water for 10-12 minutes and set aside.
2. Heat a cast iron grill pan, non-stick skillet or outdoor grill to high heat. Season both sides of the steak with black pepper. Cook each side for 4-5 minutes until medium rare. Rest the steak on a cutting board.
3. Add the garlic, onion and chicken broth to a wok, or large saucepan, on medium heat. Cook for 3-5 minutes. Add the green peppers, mushrooms and broccoli. Cover and cook for an additional 5 minutes.
4. Slice the steak against the grain then add to the vegetables. Add the drained noodles and Szechuan sauce. Stir to coat the noodles. Cover and simmer for an additional 2-3 minutes.
5. Serve hot with optional toppings and enjoy with chopsticks.

Tip: Let the protein sales at your grocery store decide your week's meals. Grill up a larger steak and use it in two or three different dishes that week; steak and eggs, steak sandwiches, steak and veggie stir fry, etc.

PEPPERONI PIZZA BAGELS

My friends always order a few pizzas after a long night out. When they're chowing down on gluten and dairy, I whip up these pizza bagels in a flash. Not only are they delicious, but they hold more nutritional value than their greasy meal.

Approximate Nutritional Information: (per bagel)

Calories: 316   Total Fat: 16 grams   Carbs: 37 grams   Protein: 9 grams

Ingredients: (Yields 4 servings)

- 1 (15 oz.) can gluten-free, no-salt-added tomato sauce
- 1 tsp. dried oregano
- 1/2 Tbsp. extra virgin olive oil
- 1 garlic clove, minced
- 4 gluten-free bagels
- 2 tsps. garlic powder
- 1/4 cup dairy-free mozzarella shreds
- 24 slices gluten-free turkey pepperoni

1. To make the pizza sauce, heat the olive oil in a saucepan on medium heat. Add the garlic and cook for 2-3 minutes. Add the tomato sauce and dried oregano. Bring to a slow boil. Cover and reduce heat to simmer.
2. Slice each bagel in half and lightly toast. If frozen, thaw completely then toast.
3. Preheat oven to broil on low. Place the toasted bagels, cut side up, onto an ungreased baking sheet. Sprinkle the garlic powder onto each bagel. Spoon on the tomato sauce, sprinkle on about 1/2 tablespoon of mozzarella and add 3 slices of turkey pepperoni to each bagel half. Broil for 6-8 minutes to melt the mozzarella and crisp the turkey pepperoni.
4. Serve with baked chicken breasts and any remaining pizza sauce.

Tip: Instead of dinner, use this recipe for an appetizer at your next gathering. Cut each bagel half into four pieces. Place one slice of turkey pepperoni on each piece. Make them with sausage, ham or vegetables for vegetarians. Substitute the mozzarella with Gouda or provolone. Your guests won't even know they are eating gluten-free.

PINEAPPLE FRIED RICE

During a vacation in Boston, I was introduced to the delicious and distinctive flavors of Thai food. Pineapple fried rice is one of the most classic Thai dishes, not to mention the tastiest. My version cuts out a lot of the fats and increases the portion size. The tender pieces of shrimp are just a bonus.

Approximate Nutritional Information: (per serving)

Calories: 284   Total Fat: 5 grams   Carbs: 47 grams   Protein: 17 grams

Ingredients: (Yields 4 servings)

- 1 cup dry kasmati style rice (or short grain white, basmati)
- 1 Tbsp. vegetable oil (or coconut oil, palm oil)
- 2 Tbsps. gluten-free reduced sodium soy sauce
- 1/2 cup yellow onion, diced
- 1 cup green bell pepper, diced
- 1/2 cup carrots, shredded
- 1/2 cup celery, diced
- 1 garlic clove, minced
- 1 Tbsp. fresh ginger, minced (or 1/2 Tbsp. ground ginger)
- 1 cup fresh pineapple, cubed
- 1 Tbsp. scallions, chopped
- 8 ounces extra large raw shrimp, cleaned, peeled, with tails removed and chopped

1. Cook the rice according to the package's instructions.
2. Heat the vegetable oil in a large pot on medium heat. Add the garlic, ginger and onion. Sauté for 3-4 minutes. Add the bell peppers, carrots and celery. Cook for an additional 5 minutes.
3. Once the vegetables are tender, add the shrimp, pineapple and scallions, reserving some scallions for garnish. Cook for 4-5 minutes until the shrimp are fully cooked.
4. Add cooked rice to the pot. Pour in soy sauce and stir until rice is coated.
5. Serve topped with remaining chopped scallions and my walnut chicken. (GlutenFreeMyRecipe.com)

Tip: Once you've tasted fresh pineapple, you'll never buy precut or canned again. Don't let it intimidate you. All you need is a sharp knife to remove the skin and core. Store leftover pineapple cubes or slices in a plastic container for a snack or tossed in a salad. Freeze some pineapple cubes and add them to a morning smoothie with ice, unsweetened almond milk and fresh strawberries.

PISTACHIO PESTO CRUSTED CHICKEN BREAST

After making this sauce, I will never purchase jarred pesto again. I like knowing what is in my food. Plus, there is something about fresh basil and nuts in a food processor that drives my senses wild. Pesto is normally made with pine nuts. Considering their high cost and a big bag of pistachios, my favorite nut, is always in my pantry, I did a switcheroo.

Approximate Nutritional Information: (per 4 oz. chicken)

Calories: 275   Total Fat: 16 grams   Carbs: 7 grams   Protein: 30 grams

Ingredients: (Yields 4 servings)

- 16 ounces antibiotic-free, boneless chicken breasts, sliced thin
- 2 Tbsps. extra virgin olive oil
- Juice from 1 lemon
- 1/2 Tbsp. lemon zest
- 1 Tbsp. dairy-free grated Parmesan (or regular Parmesan)
- 1 garlic clove
- 1 cup (packed) fresh basil leaves
- 1/2 cup unsalted shelled pistachios
- Coconut oil spray

1. In a food processor, add the extra virgin olive oil, lemon juice, lemon zest, grated Parmesan, garlic clove, basil and shelled pistachios. Pulse the mixture until the pistachios are broken into small pieces.
2. Marinate the thinly sliced chicken breasts with the pesto mixture in an airtight plastic container and refrigerate overnight.
3. When ready to serve, preheat oven to 375° F. Place the chicken on a baking sheet lined with foil and coated with non-stick coconut oil spray. Cover each chicken breast top liberally with the pesto mixture. Bake for 15-20 minutes, pesto side up.
4. Broil on high for an additional 5 minutes, until the pesto crust is brown.
5. Serve chicken with one serving of quick garlic and oil pasta. Sauté 3 garlic cloves (minced) in 1/3 cup extra virgin olive oil on medium heat. Coat 8 ounces of your favorite gluten-free pasta (cooked and drained) in the garlic and oil. Top with 1/4 cup of dairy-free grated Parmesan.

Tip: Buy unsalted or raw nuts on sale or in the bulk section of your local health market. Toast your nuts at home in a 325° F oven, on a greased baking sheet until golden brown. For a spicy nut blend, coat with smoked paprika, cayenne pepper and garlic powder.

PULLED PORK MACHO NACHOS

I used to scarf down an entire platter of nachos by myself, and that was just an appetizer. This is my number one "cheat meal", but it's healthy enough to indulge in every day. Slowly cooked pork with onions and spices, piled high on tortilla chips, globed with cheesy, mouthwatering goodness. This is ideal for Sunday football.

Approximate Nutritional Information: (per serving)

Calories: 476   Total Fat: 14 grams   Carbs: 35 grams   Protein: 42 grams

Ingredients: (Yields 4 servings)

- 24 ounces organic boneless center-cut pork loin
- 1 (16 oz.) jar organic medium salsa
- 4 servings gluten-free corn tortilla chips
- 1 cup dairy-free cheddar shreds (or regular cheddar)
- 1 cup lettuce, shredded
- 2 plum tomatoes, diced
- 1 jalapeno pepper (or serrano, habanero), sliced
- 1/4 cup dairy-free sour cream (or regular sour cream)

1. In a slow cooker, crock-pot or large pot, add the pork and the jar of salsa. Cover and cook on low for 2-3 hours, until the pork is fall apart tender. Check periodically to make sure the pork is fully covered with liquid. Add additional water, or chicken stock, if necessary.
2. Preheat your oven's broiler to low. Pull the pork apart with a fork and mix well with the remaining liquid from the slow cooker.
3. Portion out four single servings of chips onto an ungreased baking tray and top with the pork mixture. Sprinkle the cheddar on top. Broil the nachos on low for 5-7 minutes, until the pork has crusted, and the cheddar has melted.
4. Serve each plate of nachos topped with the cold toppings; tomatoes, lettuce, sour cream and jalapenos.

Tip: Not a fan of Mexican style nachos? Substitute the pork for shredded beef or chicken and replace the salsa with gluten-free BBQ sauce. Top with chopped scallions and gluten-free ranch dressing. For a vegetarian alternative, top gluten-free veggie chips with my BBQ baked beans and dairy-free coleslaw (GlutenFreeMyRecipe.com). Try making your own chips by cutting up a gluten-free spinach wrap or pita. Bake in a 400° F oven, on a pizza stone or baking sheet, until crispy.

ROSEMARY PORK CHOPS AND APPLE SLAW

Did you know according to the USDA, each American consumes over sixty pounds of pork a year? I'm way past that average. Pork chops, like chicken breasts, take on any flavors you infuse with them. Don't underestimate the simplicity of fresh rosemary, sea salt and black pepper. It's a winner.

Approximate Nutritional Information: (per 4 oz. pork and one serving of slaw)

Calories: 244   Total Fat: 10 grams   Carbs: 20 grams   Protein: 24 grams

Ingredients: (Yields 4 servings)

- 16 ounces organic, boneless center-cut pork chops, 1 1/2 inches thick
- 2 Tbsps. fresh rosemary, chopped (or 1 Tbsp. dried rosemary)
- 1 tsp. garlic powder
- 1 tsp. freshly ground black pepper
- 1/2 tsp. freshly ground sea salt
- *Apple slaw:* 1/4 cup apple cider vinegar, 1/4 cup reduced fat vegan mayo, 1/4 cup Dijon mustard, 2 medium Macintosh apples (peeled and julienned), 4 cups cabbage (shredded), 1 large carrot (peeled and julienned) and 1/4 tsp. freshly ground sea salt.

1. Remove any visible fat from the pork chops. Add rosemary, garlic, sea salt and black pepper with the pork chops to a plastic storage container and refrigerate for at least 1 hour.
2. Cook the chops on a cast iron grill pan, or outdoor grill, on high heat. After 2-3 minutes, turn the chops 90° to achieve cross-hatching grill marks. Cook an additional 2-3 minutes, flip then repeat for the other side.
3. Finish cooking the pork chops in a 400° F oven for an additional 5-10 minutes. [USDA guidelines state that pork is safe for consumption when cooked to an internal temperature of 145° F.] Remove from the oven and let rest.
4. To make the apple slaw, combine all ingredients in a small bowl. Coat well. For best results, refrigerate overnight.
5. Serve pork chops over a bed of mixed greens, alongside a vegetable medley and cold apple slaw.

Tip: If you prefer, serve with my apple compote recipe. Add diced apples of your choice to a medium sized non-stick pan, on medium heat. Sprinkle the apples with organic cane sugar or your favorite sweetener. Cook until the apples are caramelized and tender. Serve hot.

SHRIMP "DON'T SKIMP ON THE" SCAMPI

Shrimp is a new addition to my diet. When I was four-years-old, I was rushed to the hospital for a severe allergic reaction after eating mussels. I was advised by my doctor to avoid all seafood. Recently, I learned shrimp was no longer on my allergy list. Now that I'm able to experiment with shrimp, scampi has become one of my favorites. Garlic, butter and wine... Need I say more?

Approximate Nutritional Information: (per 4 oz. shrimp)

Calories: 333   Total Fat: 9 grams   Carbs: 23 grams   Protein: 39 grams

Ingredients: (Yields 4 servings)

- 16 ounces extra large shrimp, cleaned, peeled with tails on
- 2 Tbsps. vegan butter (or unsalted butter)
- 4 garlic cloves, minced
- Juice from 1 lemon
- 1 Tbsp. lemon zest
- 2 Tbsps. fresh flat-leaf parsley, chopped
- 1/4 tsp. freshly ground sea salt
- 1 tsp. freshly ground white peppercorns
- 2 oz. dry white wine (Pinot Grigio, Sauvignon Blanc)
- 1 (8 oz.) package soybean spaghetti (or your favorite gluten-free spaghetti, linguini)

1. Cook the spaghetti according to the package's instructions.
2. Pat shrimp dry on paper towels. Melt the butter in a large pan, on medium heat. Add the shrimp in small batches (do not crowd the pan) and cook for 2-3 minutes on each side. Repeat the process for all of the shrimp and set aside.
3. Add the garlic to the remaining liquid in the pan and turn heat to medium-high. Deglaze the pan with a splash of white wine, scraping the brown bits from the bottom. Turn the heat to simmer and return the shrimp to the pan. Add the lemon juice, lemon zest, sea salt and white pepper.
4. Serve one-forth of scampi hot over one serving of spaghetti and top with freshly chopped parsley.

Tip: When melting the butter, make sure your pan is not too hot. Burning butter or garlic with leave a distinct bitter or burnt taste in the dish. No harm in making errors in the kitchen, but if you do end up burning it, make sure you start from scratch. Shrimp scampi can also taste wonderful served over rice.

SIZZLING SKILLET CHICKEN FAJITAS

People tend to view fajitas as the healthier option on Mexican restaurant menus. In reality, when you add the cheese, sour cream, salsa, guacamole and tortillas, it's not the most nutritious and calorie friendly meal. For my fajitas, I replace the unhealthy toppings with nutritious ones, and let the chicken and vegetables shine like the main attraction.

Approximate Nutritional Information: (per fajitas serving and two tortillas)

Calories: 453   Total Fat: 15 grams   Carbs: 47 grams   Protein: 36 grams

Ingredients: (Yields 4 servings)

- 16 ounces antibiotic-free, boneless chicken breasts
- 2 large bell peppers (1 green, 1 red), julienned
- 1 medium yellow onion, julienned
- 8 gluten-free plain tortillas
- 1 cup dairy-free cheddar shreds (or regular cheddar)
- 1 cup plum tomatoes, diced
- 1 cup iceberg lettuce, shredded
- 1 Tbsp. extra virgin olive oil (or canola, vegetable)
- *Fajita spices:* 1 tsp. each; ground cumin, chili powder, paprika, garlic powder and onion powder. 1/2 tsp. each; freshly ground sea salt, freshly ground black pepper and cayenne pepper
- *Optional toppings:* 1/4 cup dairy-free sour cream, 1/2 cup cucumbers (sliced), 1/4 cup organic medium salsa.

1. Remove any visible fat from the chicken breasts. In a small bowl, combine all fajita spices. Coat the chicken breasts with spice mixture. Heat the olive oil in a cast-iron fajita skillet on medium-high heat. Cook the chicken breasts and set aside.
2. In the same skillet, cook the bell peppers and onions until tender.
3. Slice the chicken breasts into thin strips. Heat the tortillas, on a paper towel, in the microwave for 15-20 seconds.
4. Serve the chicken, vegetables, optional toppings and tortillas as a "create-your-own fajita" bar.

Tip: If you're dining out, don't be afraid to call ahead and ask if they provide healthy substitutions. Some places will be happy to accommodate you with lettuce wraps instead of tortillas. Skip the high-fat cheddar and guacamole. Bulk up each wrap with extra vegetables. Use salsa as your main condiment and, jazz it up with hot sauce.

SPINACH AND FETA CHICKEN ROLL UPS WITH OLIVE DIPPING SAUCE

I always wondered why the fried stuffed chicken breasts at my local Greek diner made my stomach do flip-flops. I can no longer indulge in that delicious dish, but I can still appreciate its Greek flavors. Since I'm lactose intolerant, I replace the feta cheese for a dairy-free soy alternative and eliminated the fried coating.

Nutritional Information: (per 4 oz. chicken)

Calories: 151   Total Fat: 2 grams   Carbs: 3 grams   Protein: 28 grams

Ingredients: (Yields 4 servings)

- 16 ounces antibiotic-free, boneless chicken breasts
- 4 cups organic baby spinach
- 4 ounces soy feta (or 1/4 cup light feta cheese)
- 1 Tbsp. paprika
- 1/2 tsp. freshly ground black pepper
- 1/4 tsp. freshly ground sea salt
- Gluten-free non-stick spray
- Toothpicks
- *Olive dipping sauce:* 1 cup organic baby spinach, 2 ounces soy feta (or 2 Tbsps. light feta cheese), 1/2 cup dairy-free cream cheese (or sour cream, yogurt), 1/4 cup kalamata olives (chopped), 2 ounces roasted red peppers (chopped), 1/2 tsp. garlic powder, 1/2 tsp. freshly ground white peppercorns and 1/4 tsp. freshly ground sea salt.

1. Preheat oven to 450° F. Remove any visible fat from the chicken breasts and cut them into quarter inch slices.
2. Add 5 cups of baby spinach to 1 cup of water in a large pot, on medium heat. Cook until wilted. Drain, let cool then chop. Reserve one-fifth for the dipping sauce.
3. Spoon the spinach and sprinkle soy feta on each chicken slice. Roll lengthwise then secure with a toothpick. Place on a baking sheet lined with foil and coated with non-stick spray.
4. Sprinkle each roll up with paprika and bake for 20-25 minutes.
5. For dipping sauce, combine all ingredients with the reserved spinach in a small bowl.
6. Serve roll ups hot with a side of olive dipping sauce.

Tip: Move over salsa and French onion dip. Serve the olive dipping sauce with a crudité platter at your next party. Have a second batch handy because your guests will rave.

STUFFED POBLANO PEPPERS

Would you believe me if I told you this recipe was developed by accident? I felt like adding some fresh green bell pepper to my morning veggie omelet. *Wait, these aren't bell peppers.* I must have grabbed poblanos during my erratic supermarket dash. When in doubt, stuff it.

Approximate Nutritional Information: (per pepper)

Calories: 267   Total Fat: 10 grams   Carbs: 22 grams   Protein: 29 grams

Ingredients: (Yields 4 servings)

- 16 ounces organic, lean ground turkey breast
- 4 poblano peppers
- 1/2 cup yellow onion, diced
- 2 garlic cloves, minced
- 2 medium tomatoes on the vine, diced
- 4 jalapeno peppers (seeds removed), finely chopped
- 1/2 cup dairy-free cheddar shreds
- 1 cup organic medium salsa
- *Spices:* 2 tsps. paprika, 2 tsps. onion powder, 2 tsps. garlic powder, 2 tsps. ground cumin, 1 tsp. chili powder and 1/2 tsp. cayenne pepper.
- *Optional toppings:* 1/4 cup organic medium salsa, 2 Tbsps. dairy-free sour cream, 1/2 cup lettuce (shredded), 1 Tbsp. fresh cilantro (chopped).

1. Preheat oven to 400° F. Brown the turkey in a large non-stick pan on medium-high heat. Add the onion, garlic and jalapeno. Cook for an additional 4-5 minutes. Add the diced tomatoes and the spices. Reduce heat to a simmer.
2. Slice the poblano peppers, lengthwise, and remove the seeds.
3. Coat the bottom of a medium sized baking dish with the salsa. Place the peppers in the dish, spoon the turkey mixture equally and add 2 tablespoons of cheddar onto each pepper.
4. Cover the baking dish with foil and bake for 25-30 minutes, until the peppers are tender. Remove the foil. Broil on high for an additional 5 minutes to brown the tops.
5. Serve each pepper topped with optional toppings and use gluten-free corn tortilla chips as utensils.

Tip: For very tender peppers, pour a small amount of water into the bottom of the baking dish. The more liquid in the dish, the more tender the finished product. As far as heat is concerned, poblano peppers are rather mild. Love spicy? Experiment with Fresno, Habanero or even Serrano peppers. I add some to my homemade salsa and pico de gallo.

TURKEY AND CRANBERRY "NOT SO CHILLY" CHILI

Once Thanksgiving is over, people can forget how well juicy turkey pairs with cranberries. Instead of roasting a whole bird in the oven and cracking open a can of jellied cranberry sauce, I created a chili recipe that fulfills my Thanksgiving cravings any time of year.

Approximate Nutritional Information: (per serving)

Calories: 304   Total Fat: 3 grams   Carbs: 32 grams   Protein: 36 grams

Ingredients: (Yields 4 servings)

- 16 ounces organic, lean ground turkey breast
- 1 cup gluten-free low sodium chicken broth
- 1 (15 oz.) can organic kidney beans
- 1 (28 oz.) can gluten-free, no-salt-added crushed tomatoes
- 1 medium yellow onion, diced
- 2 garlic cloves, minced
- 1/2 cup fresh cranberries (or 2 Tbsps. of dried cranberries), chopped
- *Spices:* 2 Tbsps. chili powder, 1 Tbsp. ground cumin, 1 tsp. paprika, 1/2 tsp. garlic powder, 1/2 tsp. freshly ground black pepper, 1/4 tsp. cayenne pepper and 1/4 tsp. freshly ground sea salt.
- *Optional toppings:* 2 Tbsps. raw yellow onion (chopped), 1/4 cup dairy-free Mexican shreds, 2 Tbsps. dairy-free sour cream, 1/4 cup organic medium salsa.

1. Brown the turkey in a large pot on high heat. Add the garlic and onions. Cook for 3-4 minutes, until onions are translucent.
2. Add the chicken broth, crushed tomatoes and chili spices. Bring to a boil. Cover, reduce heat to simmer and cook for at least one hour. Stir occasionally. If the chili becomes too thick, add additional chicken broth or water.
3. Drain and rinse the kidney beans with water. Add the beans and cranberries to the pot. Cover and simmer for an additional 30 minutes.
4. Serve chili over brown rice or with gluten-free tortilla chips and optional toppings.

Tip: For a spicier chili, add more cayenne pepper, chipotle flakes or chopped jalapenos with seeds. You can always put more spice but never take out, so taste after adding each spice. Try swapping the chicken broth with gluten-free beer. Refrigerate any leftover chili. It tastes even better the next day.

TURKEY ANDOUILLE SAUSAGE AND SHRIMP GUMBO

I watch a lot of cooking shows on television. Maybe more than I care to admit. I get a ton of my inspiration from looking at different recipes and dishes served at restaurants around the country. I learn to incorporate obscure ingredients in my repertoire. These Louisiana flavors will bring you straight to Bourbon Street. No beads necessary.

Approximate Nutritional Information: (per serving)

Calories: 392   Total Fat: 11 grams   Carbs: 50 grams   Protein: 26 grams

Ingredients: (Yields 4 servings)

- 1 (12 oz.) package organic turkey Andouille sausage
- 1 dozen extra large shrimp, cleaned, peeled with tails removed
- 1 Tbsp. vegan butter (or unsalted butter)
- 1 Tbsp. cornstarch (or brown rice flour, white rice flour)
- 1 cup gluten-free unsalted vegetable stock
- 1 small yellow onion, diced
- 1 medium green bell pepper, diced
- 1 garlic clove, minced
- 2 large celery stalks, diced
- 1/2 cup okra, diced
- 1 medium tomato on the vine, diced
- 1 cup organic short grain brown rice
- 2 Tbsps. scallions, chopped
- *Cajun spices:* 2 tsps. paprika, 2 tsps. garlic powder, 1 tsp. dried oregano, 1 tsp. dried thyme, 1 tsp. onion powder, 1/2 tsp. cayenne pepper, 1/2 tsp. freshly ground black pepper, 1/4 tsp. freshly ground sea salt and 1/4 tsp. red pepper flake.

1. Cook the rice according to the package's instructions.
2. Melt the butter in a large pan on medium heat. Whisk in the cornstarch to create a roux. Stir constantly until smooth and golden brown.
3. Add the onions, celery, peppers and garlic. Cook for 3-5 minutes. Slice sausage on a bias, 1/2 inch thick. Stir in the sausage, vegetable broth, tomatoes, okra and Cajun spices. Cover and simmer for an additional 5-7 minutes. Add the shrimp and simmer until fully cooked.
4. Serve gumbo hot over a serving of rice, topped with scallions.

Tip: Most gumbos are made with the trinity - onions, peppers and celery. They're also the staple ingredients for most delicious stir-fries and soups. Seafood lovers can add oysters, bay scallops, clams, crabmeat, along with shrimp, for a tasty, low-fat seafood gumbo.

VERY VEGGIE LENTIL SOUP

It's very upsetting to find out something I love to eat isn't gluten-free. This past brisk winter, I wanted to indulge in some warm and comforting vegetable soup from a popular bread chain. I learned there were tiny bits of barley concealed in my bowl. My variation is free of any off-limit grains and packed with fresh, seasonal vegetables.

Approximate Nutritional Information: (per serving)

Calories: 166   Total Fat: 4 grams   Carbs: 23 grams   Protein: 13 grams

Ingredients: (Yields 4 servings)

- 1 (4 cup) container gluten-free unsalted chicken stock
- 1 Tbsp. extra virgin olive oil
- 1 cup celery, chopped
- 1 cup carrots, chopped
- 1/2 cup zucchini, diced
- 1 cup Swiss chard, chopped
- 1 small yellow onion, diced
- 1 garlic clove, minced
- 1 plum tomato, diced
- 2 Tbsps. gluten-free organic tomato paste
- 1 (15 oz.) can organic black lentil beans
- 1 tsp. dried basil (or 1 Tbsp. fresh basil, chopped)
- 1 tsp. freshly ground black pepper
- 1/4 tsp. freshly ground sea salt

1. Heat the olive oil in a large pot, on medium heat. Add the garlic and onions and cook for 2-3 minutes. Add the rest of the chopped vegetables. Cook an additional 4-5 minutes.
2. Stir in the chicken stock, tomato paste, basil, black pepper and sea salt. Bring to a boil. Cover, reduce heat to simmer and cook for 60-90 minutes.
3. Drain and rinse the lentil beans in water. Add the beans to the soup and simmer for an additional 30 minutes.
4. Serve soup hot with a sprinkle of dairy-free grated Parmesan and a warm gluten-free roll or baguette.

Tip: Always keep a few containers of unsalted chicken stock in your pantry. Soup is a quick and nutritious dinner, lunch or midday snack. Clean out your fridge. Use any leftover beans, your favorite gluten-free grain and any extra vegetable you have to bulk up this hearty soup.

"WRAP ME UP IN BACON" SHRIMP

I have two great loves in my life... shrimp and turkey bacon. What better way to enjoy them but together? A small slice of jalapeno pepper and a dash of cayenne add the spicy kick I crave in my shrimp dishes. Don't worry about your waistline. This shrimp dish is so low in calorie you can indulge in a full plate.

Approximate Nutritional Information: (per 4 oz. shrimp)

Calories: 180   Total Fat: 6 grams   Carbs: 1 gram   Protein: 30 grams

Ingredients: (Yields 4 Servings)

- 16 ounces extra large shrimp, cleaned, peeled with tails on
- 1 cup jalapeno pepper (seeds removed), julienned
- 15 slices turkey bacon (thin and crispy), halved
- 1/4 tsp. cayenne pepper
- Toothpicks
- Gluten-free non-stick spray
- *Side salad:* 4 cups mixed greens (romaine, spinach, arugula, frisée) and 2 large beets (roasted and sliced).
- *Citrus vinaigrette:* 1/4 cup extra virgin olive oil, juice from one lemon, 1 Tbsp. lemon zest and 1/2 tsp. freshly ground white peppercorns.

1. Preheat oven to 400° F. Line a baking sheet with foil and coat with non-stick spray.
2. Dry shrimp on paper towels. Sprinkle both sides of each piece with cayenne pepper.
3. Assemble the wraps. Place a half slice of turkey bacon down on a cutting board. Lay one jalapeno slice and one piece of shrimp on the bacon. Fold the ends over and press a toothpick through the entire wrap. Place the wrap onto the baking sheet and repeat the process for all of the shrimp.
4. Bake for 8-10 minutes, flip and bake until bacon is crisp.
5. Serve shrimp with optional side salad tossed in citrus vinaigrette.

Tip: Bake leftover jalapeno slices along with the shrimp. The jalapenos will crisp and act as spicy chips or an alternative to croutons on your side salad. Some brands of turkey bacon are not gluten-free. Make it a habit to check the all of your labels. Use gluten-free tempeh bacon as a vegetarian alternative.

EXTRAS

SHOPPING GUIDE

Pastas, Breads and Grains
- Black Bean Spaghetti
- Brown Rice Lasagna Sheets
- Brown Rice Flour
- Cornstarch
- Gluten-Free Bagels
- Gluten-Free Breadcrumbs
- Gluten Free Egg Noodles
- Gluten-Free Pizza Dough
- Gluten-Free Tortillas
- Gluten-Free Tortilla Chips
- Gluten-Free Whole Grain Bread
- Kasmati Rice
- Pad Thai Rice Noodles
- Quinoa Pasta
- Short Grain Brown Rice
- Soybean Spaghetti

Spices
- Black Pepper, Freshly Ground
- Cardamom, Ground
- Cayenne Pepper
- Chili Powder
- Coriander, Ground
- Cumin, Ground
- Dried Basil
- Dried Oregano
- Dried Thyme
- Garlic Powder
- Ginger, Ground
- Onion Powder
- Paprika
- Red Pepper Flakes
- Sea Salt, Freshly Ground
- Turmeric
- White Pepper, Freshly Ground

Protein
- Antibiotic-Free Chicken Breasts
- Boneless Beef
- Buffalo Chicken Sausage
- Eggs
- Liquid Egg Whites
- Pork Chops, Center Cut
- Pork Loin, Center Cut
- Sirloin Steak
- Shrimp
- Tilapia
- Turkey Andouille Sausage
- Turkey Bacon
- Turkey Breast, Ground
- Turkey Pepperoni
- White Albacore Tuna
- Veal Cutlets

Canned and Jarred Products
- Black Beans, Organic
- Black Lentil Beans, Organic
- Black Olives
- Crushed Tomatoes, No-Salt-Added
- Corn Kernels, No-Salt-Added
- Kalamata Olives
- Kidney Beans, Organic
- Marinara Sauce
- Roasted Red Peppers, In Water
- Salsa, Organic
- Tomato Paste
- Tomato Sauce, No-Salt-Added
- Water Chestnuts

Fruit and Vegetables
- Apples
- Baby Spinach
- Basil
- Beefsteak Tomatoes
- Beets
- Bell Peppers
- Broccoli
- Cabbage
- Carrots
- Celery
- Cilantro
- Cranberries
- Cucumbers, Regular and Mini
- Dill
- Flat-Leaf Parsley
- Garlic
- Ginger
- Grape Tomatoes
- Iceberg Lettuce
- Jalapeno Peppers
- Lemons
- Mixed Greens
- Okra
- Pears
- Pineapple
- Plum Tomatoes
- Poblano Peppers
- Portabella Mushrooms
- Raisins
- Red Potatoes
- Red Onions
- Romaine Lettuce
- Rosemary
- Scallions
- Strawberries
- Swiss Chard
- Tomatoes On The Vine
- White Mushrooms
- Yellow Onions
- Yellow Zucchini Squash

Oils, Stocks and Condiments
- Apple Cider Vinegar
- Balsamic Vinegar
- BBQ Sauce
- Beef Stock, Unsalted
- Chicken Broth, Low Sodium
- Chicken Stock, Unsalted
- Coconut Creamer
- Coconut Oil
- Coconut Oil Spray
- Dijon Mustard
- Gluten-Free Non-Stick Spray
- Olive Oil, Extra Virgin
- Red Wine Vinegar
- Soy Sauce, Reduced Sodium
- Sweet Relish, No-Sugar-Added
- Szechuan Sauce
- Vegetable Oil
- Vegetable Stock, Unsalted
- White Wine, Dry

Dairy-Free Alternatives
- Cheddar Shreds
- Cream Cheese, Plain
- Mexican Blend Shreds
- Mozzarella Shreds
- Parmesan, Grated
- Sour Cream
- Soy Feta
- Swiss Slices
- Vegan Butter
- Vegan Mayo

Nuts
- Almonds, Slivered
- Pecans
- Pistachios, Unsalted

GLOSSARY OF TERMS

Antibiotic-Free: In order for the USDA to label chicken antibiotic-free or "raised without antibiotics", the flock must be raised without the use of classified antibiotics.

Broil: Cooking at high direct heat. Most conventional ovens have a broiler function. This is best used to crisp or brown foods.

Caramelize: The cooking process that results in the foods natural sugars turning brown.

Cross-hatching: The grilling process where you cook diagonally on the grill and then turn 90° to achieve hatch marks.

Deglaze: The act of adding liquid (normally wine) to a hot pan in which something has been cooked. The liquid will lift the browned bits from the bottom of the pan and incorporate with the liquid.

GMO: Genetically modified organisms. Organic products prohibit the use of GMOs.

Julienne: To cut into thin strips or matchstick pieces.

Mince: To cut into very small pieces.

Natural: The USDA states that a natural product has no artificial ingredients, colors or preservatives.

Organic: The USDA has strict guidelines in order for a food to be labeled "organic". Special methods are used on meats and produce to avoid pesticides.

Paleo: Also known as the "Caveman Diet", a Paleo Diet consists of grass-fed meats, organic vegetables, fruits and nuts. It excludes dairy, legumes, grains, refined sugars and processed oils.

Roux: A mixture of butter or some form of fat with flour or starch. Used to thicken sauces, gravies or soups.

Sauté: Cook down on medium-high heat (with butter, oil or cooking spray) until the food has browned.

Simmer: To cook below a boil.

Shredded: To cut or tare into small strips or shreds.

Sweat: Similar to sauté, sweating vegetables means to cook down on low-medium heat (with butter, oil or cooking spray) until the vegetables are softened. They do not turn brown or caramelize.

MEASUREMENTS AND FLOUR BLENDS

Tbsp. = Tablespoon
tsp. = teaspoon
1 Tablespoon = 3 teaspoons
2 Tablespoons = 1 fluid ounce
4 Tablespoons = 1/4 cup
16 Tablespoons = 1 cup

Oz. = Ounce
lb. = Pound
16 ounces = 1 pound
8 fluid ounces = 1 cup
1 pint = 2 cups
1 quart = 2 pints

Common gluten-free all-purpose flour blend: (yields 5 cups)
- 1 cup white rice flour or brown rice flour
- 1 cup sorghum flour or oat flour
- 1 cup tapioca flour/starch
- 1 cup cornstarch or potato starch
- 1 cup almond flour or coconut flour

(Add 1/2 tsp. xanthan gum per cup of flour)

Common gluten-free self-rising flour blend: (yields 1 cup)
- 1 cup gluten-free all-purpose flour blend
- 4 tsps. baking powder
- 1/2 tsp. salt

(Add 1/2 tsp. xanthan gum per cup of flour)

Common gluten-free pastry flour blend: (yields 5 cups)
- 2 cups white rice flour or brown rice flour
- 1 1/2 cups tapioca flour/starch
- 1 cup cornstarch
- 1/2 cup millet flour

(Add 1 tsp. xanthan gum per cup of flour)

Make your own gluten-free all-purpose flour blend:
- 2 parts of one or a combination of the following flours; buckwheat, corn, millet, oat, quinoa, sorghum, teff
- 2 parts of one of a combination of the following starches; corn, potato, tapioca
- 1 part of one of a combination of the following flours; almond, cashew, coconut, garbanzo bean

(Add 1/2 tsp. xanthan gum per cup of flour)

Made in the USA
San Bernardino, CA
19 August 2014